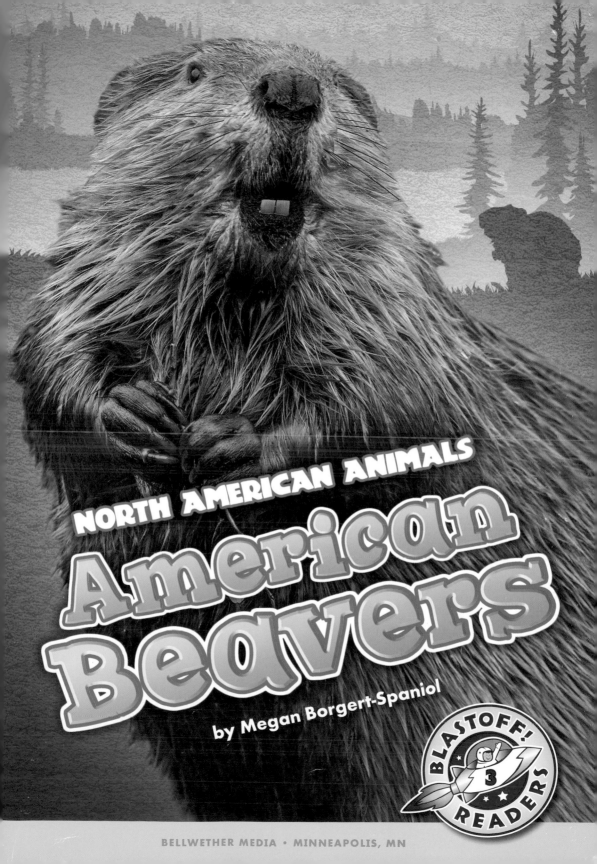

NORTH AMERICAN ANIMALS

American Beavers

by Megan Borgert-Spaniol

BLASTOFF! READERS 3

BELLWETHER MEDIA • MINNEAPOLIS, MN

Note to Librarians, Teachers, and Parents:

Blastoff! Readers are carefully developed by literacy experts and combine standards-based content with developmentally appropriate text.

Level 1 provides the most support through repetition of high-frequency words, light text, predictable sentence patterns, and strong visual support.

Level 2 offers early readers a bit more challenge through varied simple sentences, increased text load, and less repetition of high-frequency words.

Level 3 advances early-fluent readers toward fluency through increased text and concept load, less reliance on visuals, longer sentences, and more literary language.

Level 4 builds reading stamina by providing more text per page, increased use of punctuation, greater variation in sentence patterns, and increasingly challenging vocabulary.

Level 5 encourages children to move from "learning to read" to "reading to learn" by providing even more text, varied writing styles, and less familiar topics.

Whichever book is right for your reader, Blastoff! Readers are the perfect books to build confidence and encourage a love of reading that will last a lifetime!

This edition first published in 2016 by Bellwether Media, Inc.

No part of this publication may be reproduced in whole or in part without written permission of the publisher. For information regarding permission, write to Bellwether Media, Inc., Attention: Permissions Department, 5357 Penn Avenue South, Minneapolis, MN 55419.

Library of Congress Cataloging-in-Publication Data

Borgert-Spaniol, Megan, 1989- author.
  American Beavers / by Megan Borgert-Spaniol.
    pages cm. – (Blastoff! Readers. North American Animals)
  Summary: "Simple text and full-color photography introduce beginning readers to American beavers. Developed by literacy experts for students in kindergarten through third grade"– Provided by publisher.
  Audience: Ages 5-8
  Audience: K to grade 3
  Includes bibliographical references and index.
  ISBN 978-1-62617-256-2 (hardcover: alk. paper)
  1. American beaver–Juvenile literature. 2. Beavers–Juvenile literature. I. Title.
  QL737.R632B67 2016
  599.37–dc23
                                              2015000516

Printed in the United States of America, North Mankato, MN.

Table of Contents

What Are American Beavers?

American beavers are the largest **rodents** in North America. They are found throughout most of the United States and Canada.

In the Wild

N
W • E
S

Extinct

Extinct in the Wild

Critically Endangered

Endangered

Vulnerable

Near Threatened

Least Concern

American beaver range = ☐

conservation status: least concern

These **mammals** make their homes in forested areas along streams, rivers, ponds, and lakes.

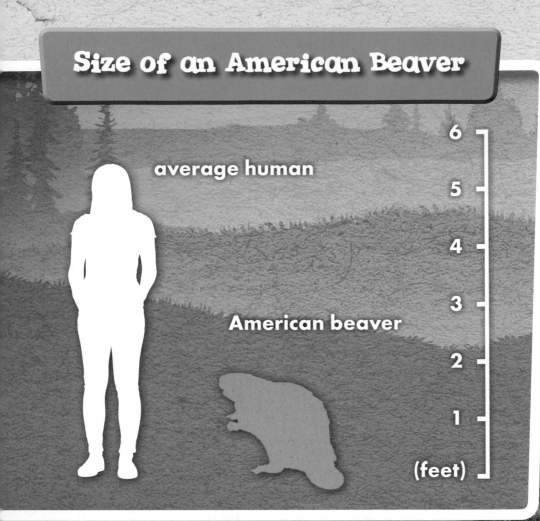

Size of an American Beaver

average human

American beaver

6
5
4
3
2
1
(feet)

American beavers are between 3 and 4 feet (0.9 and 1.2 meters) long.

Their tails are about 1 foot (0.3 meters) of this length.

Built for Water

Thick fur keeps American beavers warm in cold water.

Identify an American Beaver

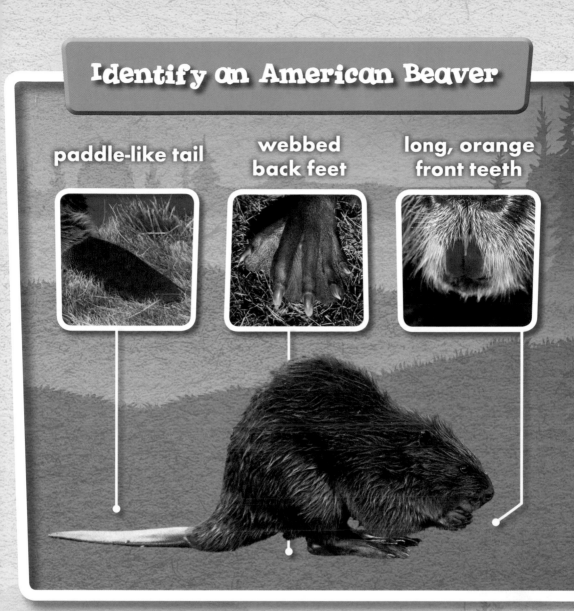

paddle-like tail

webbed back feet

long, orange front teeth

Their long outer hairs are **waterproof**. Short inner hairs trap heat against their bodies.

The beavers can stay underwater for more than 10 minutes.

Special flaps cover their ears and noses. Clear eyelids protect their eyes.

The beavers push through water with strong back legs and **webbed feet**.

Their large, flat tails help them **steer**.

Tree Eaters

American beavers are **herbivores**. They waddle onto land to eat tree bark, twigs, and leaves.

On the Menu

aspen trees

maple trees

birch trees

willow trees

white water lilies

cattails

They also eat plants that grow in water.

Dams and Lodges

The beavers gather wood to build **dams** and **lodges**. They use their long front teeth to cut into tree trunks.

Then they drag the logs and branches into the water.

Beaver dams slow the flow of water in a river or stream. This creates a pond of still water where beavers build their lodge. A lodge is home to a **colony** of parents and **kits**.

Baby Facts

Name for babies:	kits
Size of litter:	3 or 4 kits
Length of pregnancy:	about 3 to 4 months
Time spent with parents:	2 years

Animals to Avoid

gray wolves

wolverines

black bears

river otters

Together, beavers watch out for **predators**. They slap the water with their tails to warn one another of danger!

Glossary

colony—a family of beavers

dams—tall mounds made of logs, branches, mud, and stones; beavers build dams so they can build lodges.

herbivores—animals that only eat plants

kits—baby beavers

lodges—shelters made of branches and mud; beavers enter their lodges from underwater.

mammals—warm-blooded animals that have backbones and feed their young milk

predators—animals that hunt other animals for food

rodents—small animals that gnaw on their food

steer—to change direction

waterproof—able to keep water from soaking through

webbed feet—feet with thin skin that connects the toes

To Learn More

AT THE LIBRARY

Gibbons, Gail. *Beavers*. New York, N.Y.: Holiday House, 2013.

Peterson, Megan Cooley. *Look Inside a Beaver's Lodge*. Mankato, Minn.: Capstone Press, 2012.

Sill, Cathryn P. *About Rodents: A Guide for Children*. Atlanta, Ga.: Peachtree, 2008.

ON THE WEB

Learning more about American beavers is as easy as 1, 2, 3.

1. Go to www.factsurfer.com.

2. Enter "American beavers" into the search box.

3. Click the "Surf" button and you will see a list of related web sites.

With factsurfer.com, finding more information is just a click away.

Index